Tell More
Robots

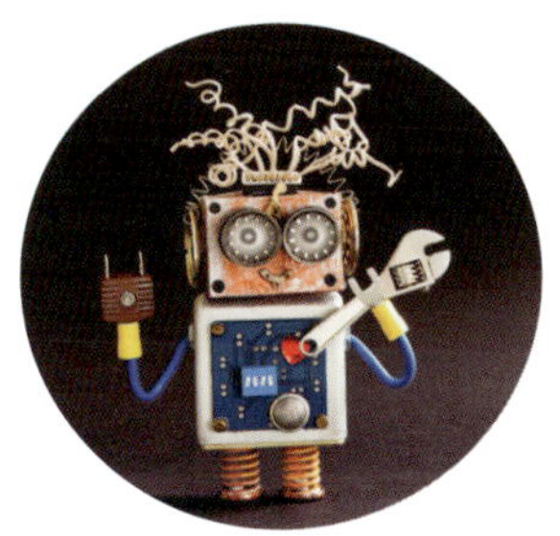

Written by
Stephen Rickard

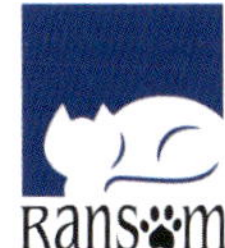

Ransom

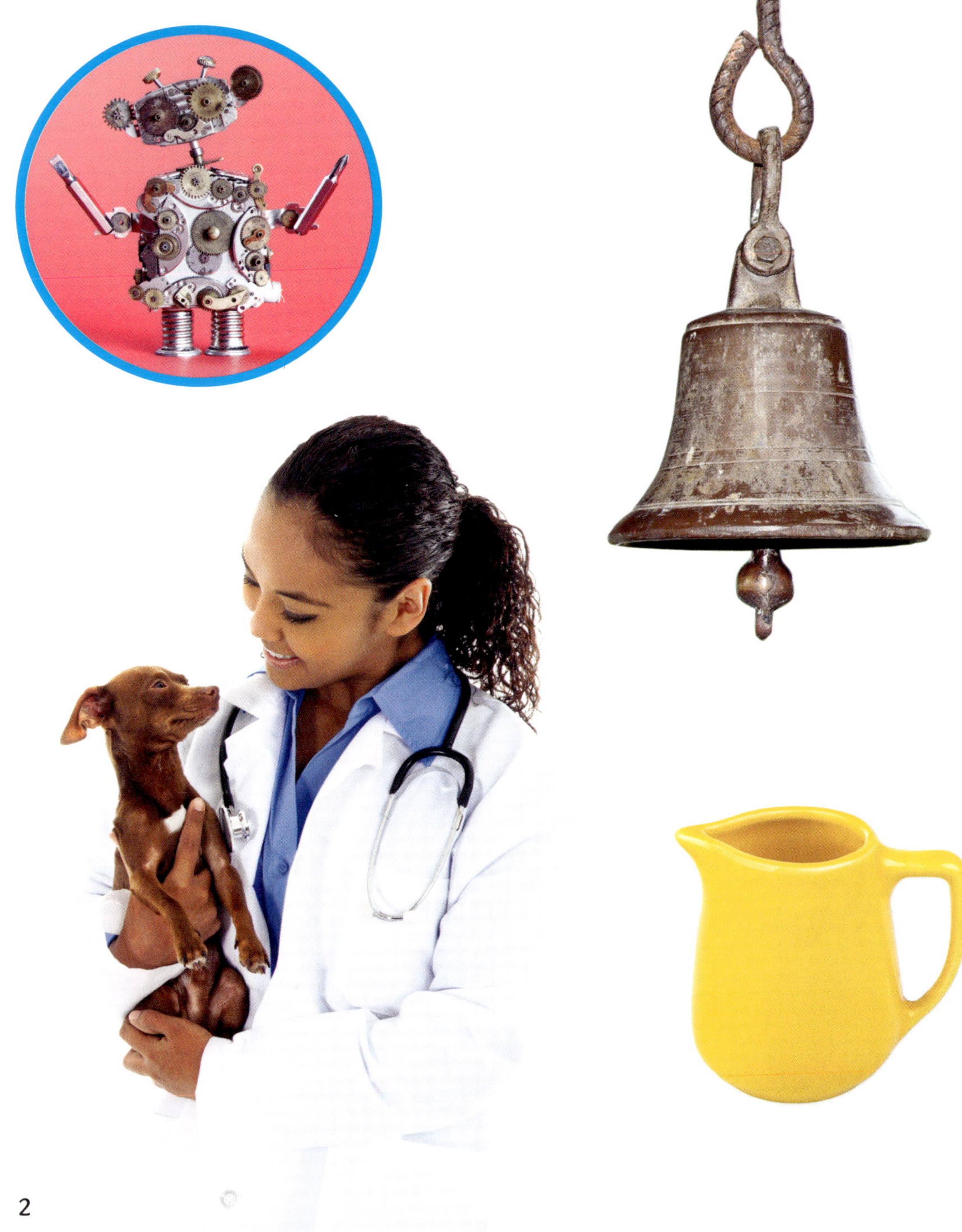

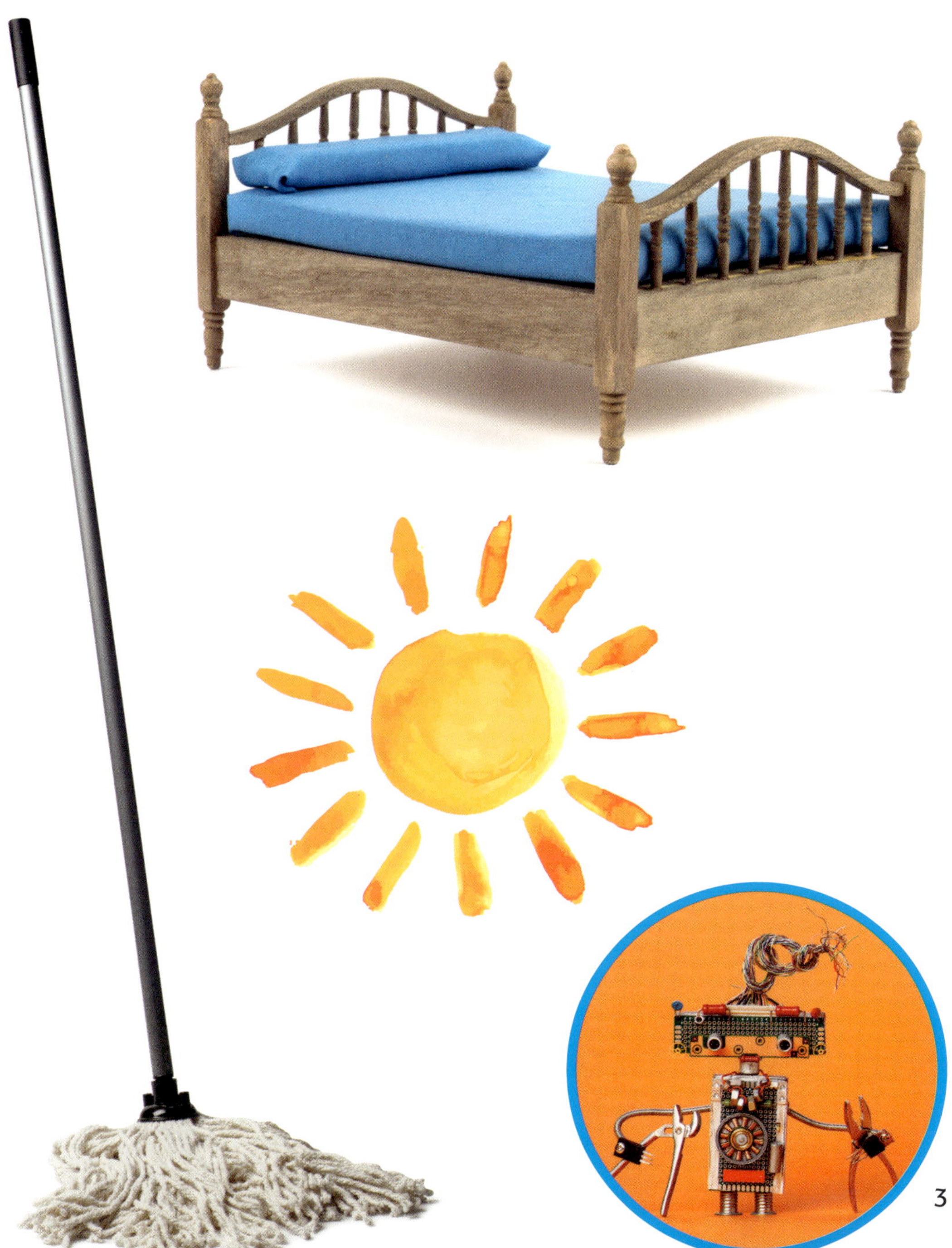

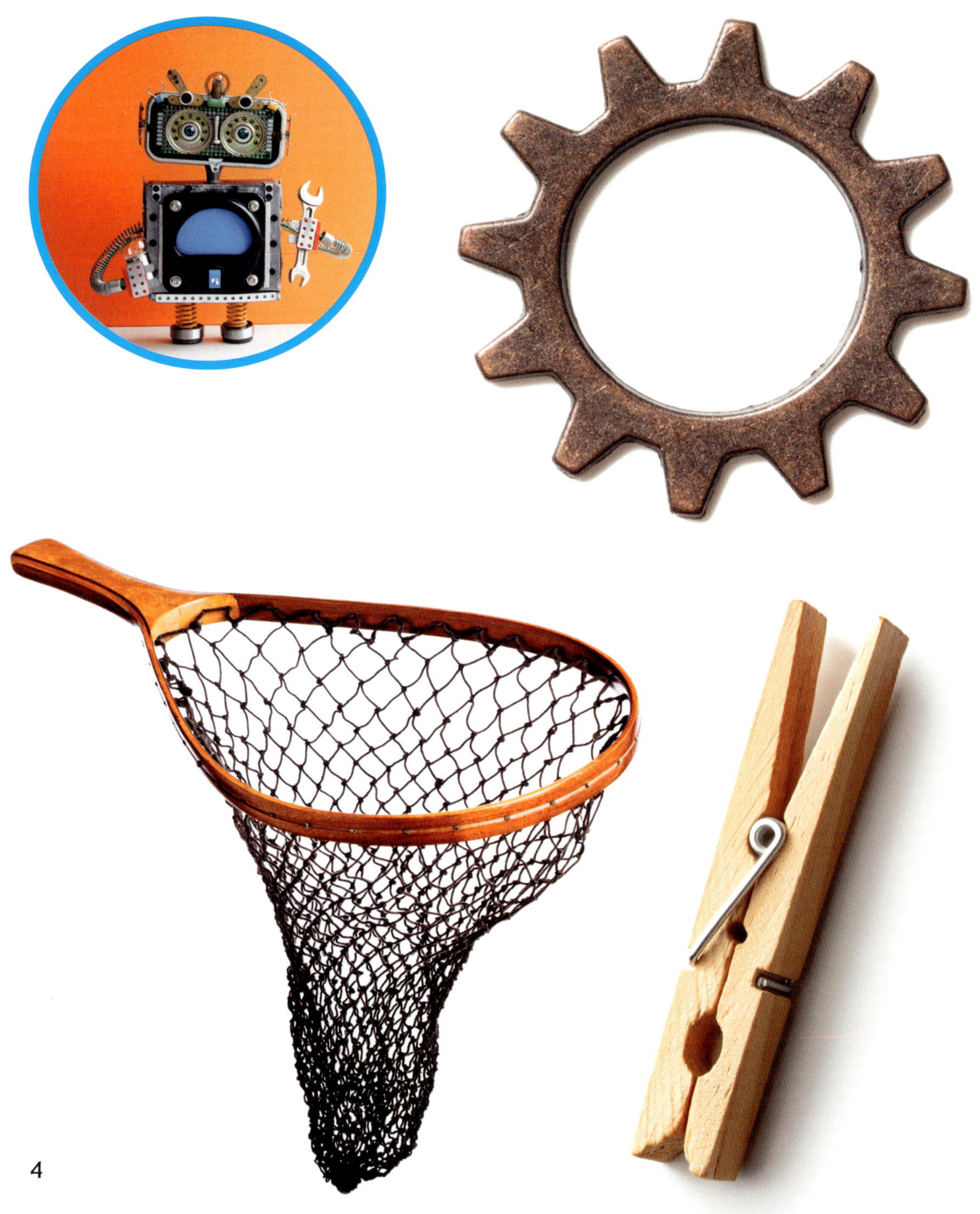

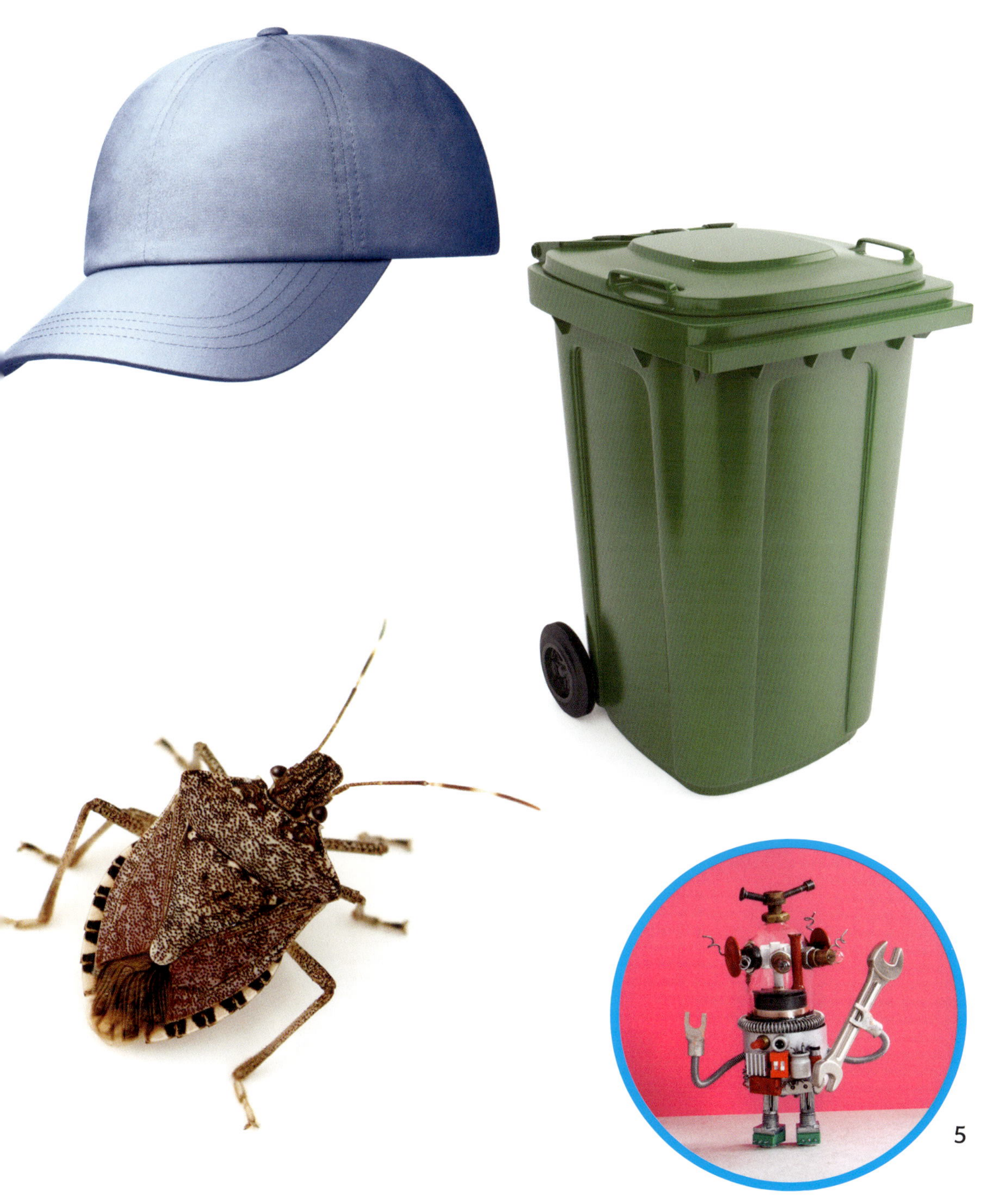

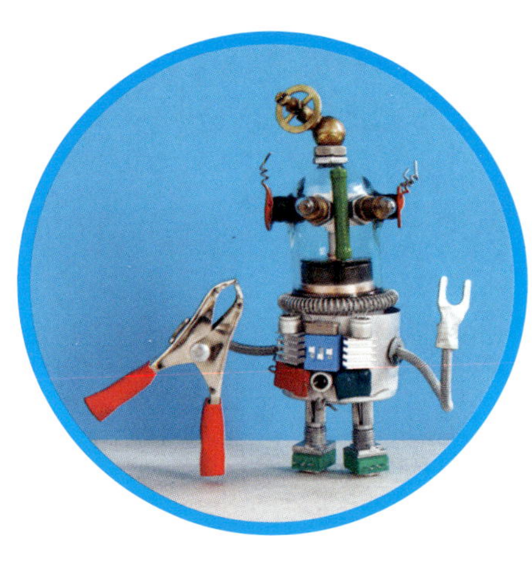

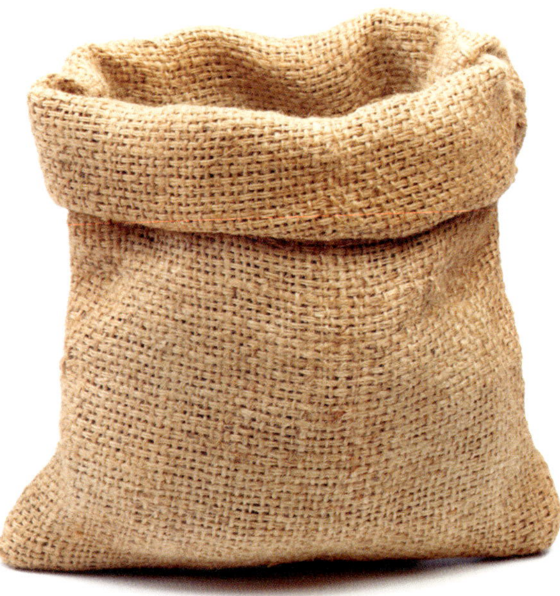

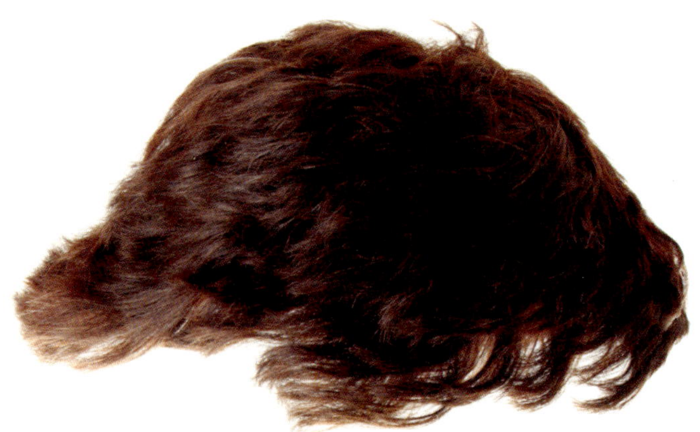

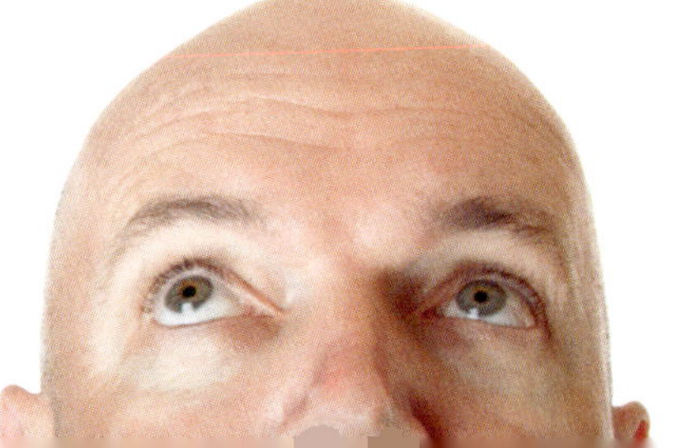

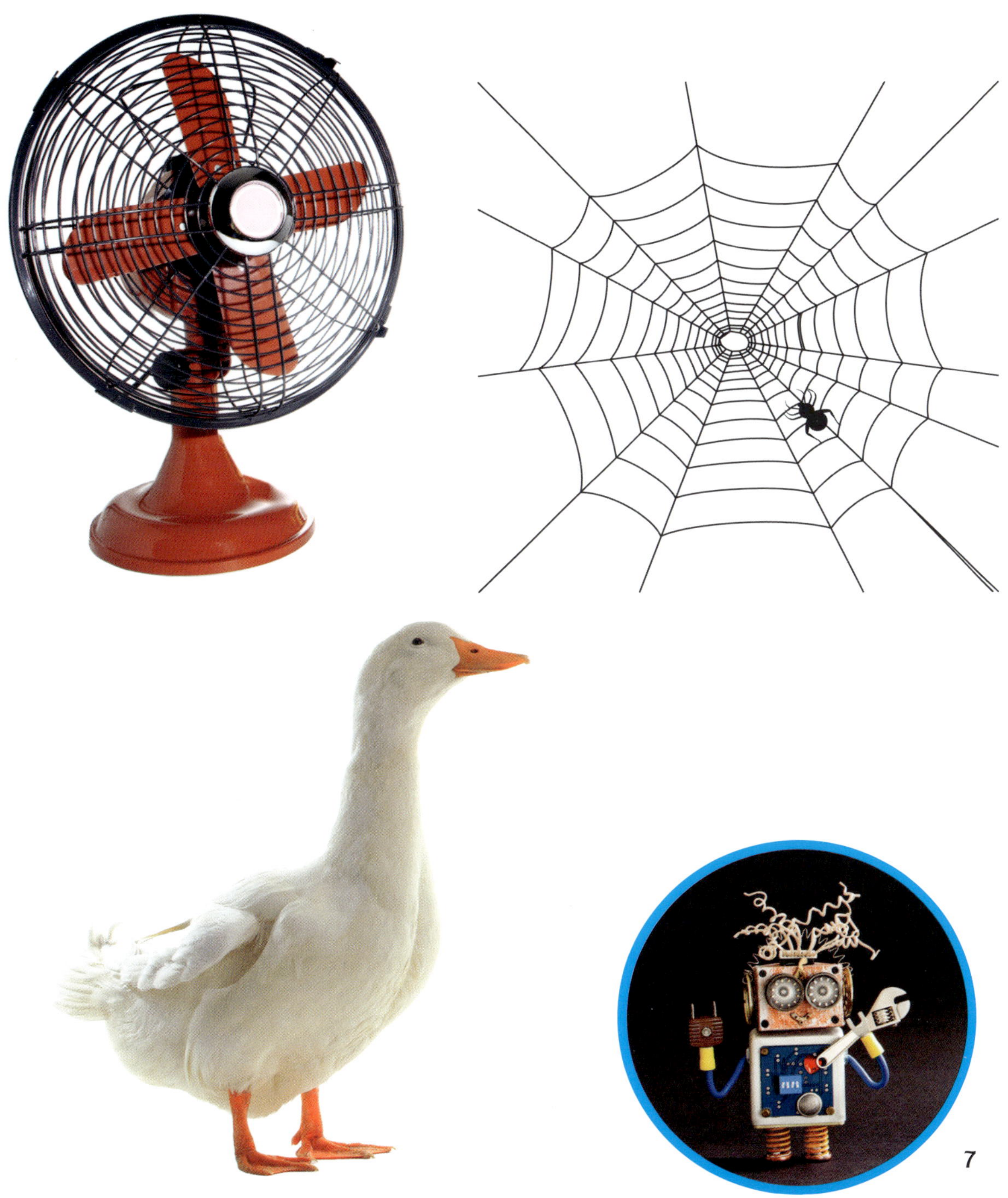

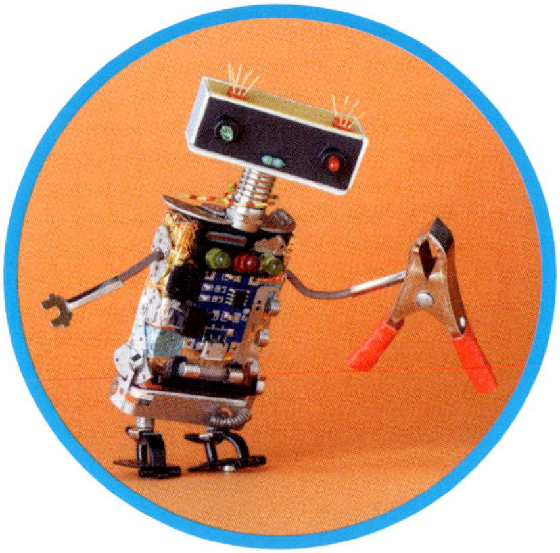

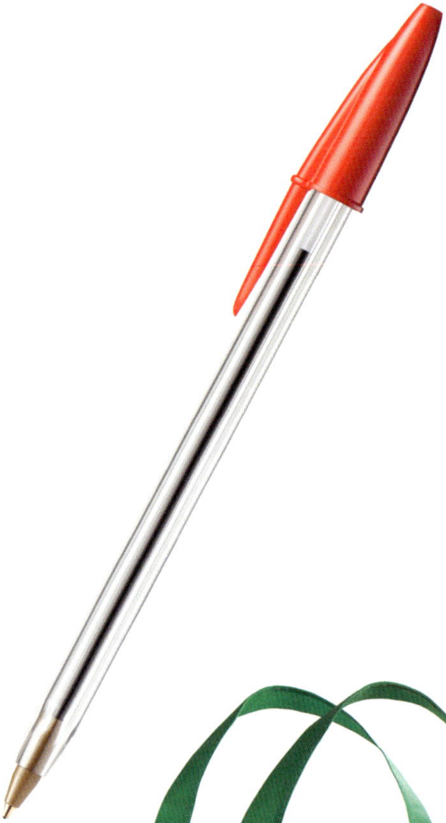

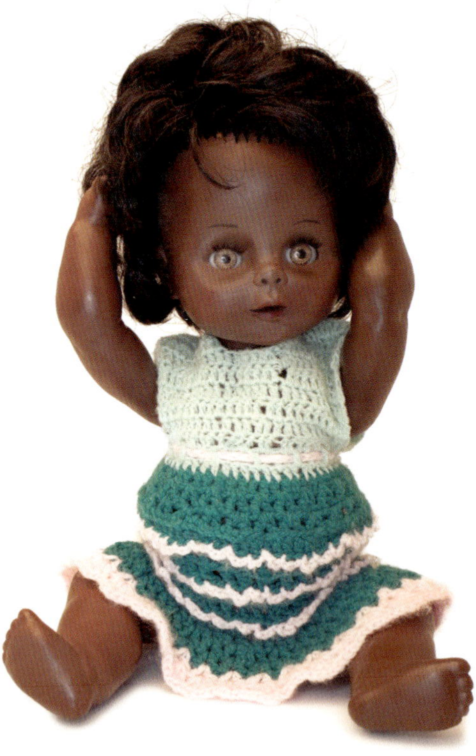

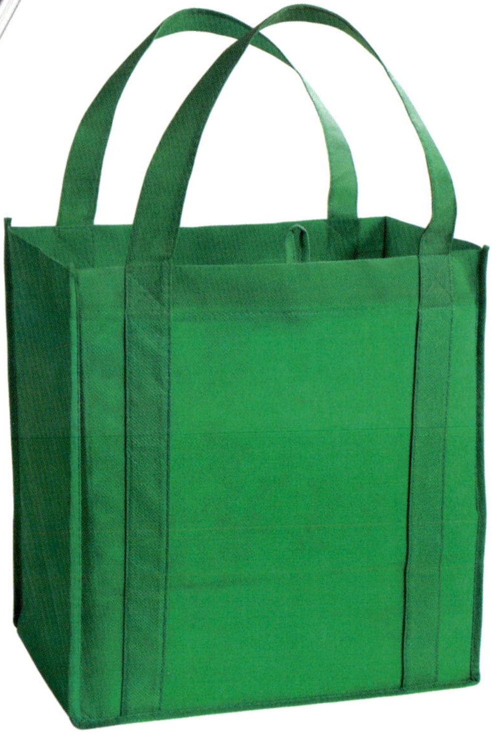